Parent's Introduction

We Both Read is the first series of books designed to invite parents and children to share the reading of a story by taking turns reading aloud. This "shared reading" innovation, which was developed with reading education specialists, invites parents to read the more complex text and storyline on the left-hand pages. Then, children can be encouraged to read the right-hand pages, which feature less complex text and storyline, specifically written for the beginning reader.

Reading aloud is one of the most important activities parents can share with their child to assist them in their reading development. However, *We Both Read* goes beyond reading *to* a child and allows parents to share the reading *with* a child. *We Both Read* is so powerful and effective because it combines two key elements in learning: "modeling" (the parent reads) and "doing" (the child reads). The result is not only faster reading development for the child, but a much more enjoyable and enriching experience for both!

You may find it helpful to read the entire book aloud yourself the first time, then invite your child to participate in the second reading. In some books, a few more difficult words will first be introduced in the parent's text, distinguished with **bold lettering**. Pointing out, and even discussing, these words will help familiarize your child with them and help to build your child's vocabulary. Also, note that a "talking parent" icon ☺ precedes the parent's text and a "talking child" icon ☺ precedes the child's text.

We encourage you to share and interact with your child as you read the book together. If your child is having difficulty, you might want to mention a few things to help them. "Sounding out" is good, but it will not work with all words. Children can pick up clues about the words they are reading from the story, the context of the sentence, or even the pictures. Some stories have rhyming patterns that might help. It might also help them to touch the words with their finger as they read, to better connect the voice sound and the printed word.

Sharing the *We Both Read* books together will engage you and your child in an interactive adventure in reading! It is a fun and easy way to encourage and help your child to read—and a wonderful way to start them off on a lifetime of reading enjoyment!

We Both Read: Wild Animals of the United States

Text Copyright © 2009 by Dev Ross
Illustrations Copyright © 2009 by the Hautman Brothers

HAUTMAN BROTHERS
C O L L E C T I O N

We Both Read® is a trademark of Treasure Bay, Inc.

Published by Treasure Bay, Inc.
40 Sir Francis Drake Boulevard
San Anselmo, CA 94960 USA

Printed in Singapore

Library of Congress Catalog Card Number: 2008929048

Hardcover ISBN-10: 1-60115-233-7
Hardcover ISBN-13: 978-1-60115-233-6
Paperback ISBN-10: 1-60115-234-5
Paperback ISBN-13: 978-1-60115-234-3

We Both Read® Books
Patent No. 5,957,693

Visit us online at:
www.webothread.com

Wild Animals
of the United States

By Dev Ross

Illustrated by the Hautman Brothers

TREASURE BAY

The United States is a vast and beautiful place where many different kinds of **wild** animals live. They live in mountains and forests, on open prairies, and even in rivers. Some even live in our own backyards.

   **Wild** animals are not like our pets. It is up to us to feed and take care of our pets. **Wild** animals find their own food and take care of themselves.

The place where a wild animal lives and finds food is called its **habitat**. As the **human** population grows, we are taking up more and more of the **habitat** of wild animals. By helping to protect our forests and other **habitats**, we can help to ensure that wild animals will always have a place to live and take care of themselves.

These bears live in the wild. **Humans** have come into the bears' **habitat** for a picnic. Now the bears are trying to eat the picnic food. This is not safe for the **humans** or the bears!

 Much of the western part of the United States was once covered in vast grassy plains, but most of these plains are now gone. On some of the plains that still exist, wild horses, called mustangs, still roam. Wild mustangs live in a large group called a **herd**. The leader of the **herd** is a male horse called a stallion. A mare is a female horse. A horse under one year old is called a **foal**.

A **foal** is able to stand and run just a few hours after it is born. Its mother, and the rest of the **herd**, will keep the **foal** safe.

You might call this animal a buffalo, but that name really only applies to the Asian water buffalo and the African buffalo. The correct name for this North **American** plains dweller is **bison**. **Bison** are wandering grazers that travel in herds. Unfortunately, in the 19th and 20th centuries these huge mammals were almost hunted to extinction.

A long time ago, **American** Indians hunted **bison** for food. They used the hide to make their homes. **Bison** were a very important part of their lives.

Herds of deer can be found high in the mountains where lush
forests surround peaceful meadows. Deer are sometimes hunted
by people who prize their meat as food and their **antlers** as trophies.
Male deer are the only deer with **antlers**. Because of the loss of
their habitat, a deer just might sneak into your garden to nibble
away at your flowers and vegetables.

Baby deer are called fawns. They are born with white spots on their fur, but when they get older they will lose their spots. You will not find **antlers** on a baby deer or its mother.

Some of us may never see a bison or a deer up close, but just outside our window we can see some of nature's most beautiful creatures. Wild birds come in brilliant reds, yellows, oranges, and blues as well as many other colors. Many wild birds sing beautiful songs. One of these beautiful songbirds is the **cardinal**.

 The **cardinal** likes to live where there are lots of flowers and trees. That is why most of them live in the woods. Sometimes you may find them living where people live.

   The great horned owl is the most widespread owl in North America. In the United States, this owl can be found living anywhere from the southwestern deserts to the Rocky Mountains in the north. These birds don't sing like the cardinal. Instead they make a hooting sound.

Great horned owls are very large birds. The smallest bird is a type of **hummingbird**.

The **hummingbird** flaps its wings very fast. The wings flap so fast that they make a sound like a hum. Did you know the **hummingbird** can fly backwards?

Moose live in dense forest areas and around lakes and streams in Alaska, Canada, and the northern United States from Washington state across to northern New England. They also live in the northern Rockies all the way south to Utah. **Moose** are strong swimmers and they will thrust their large heads **underwater** to pull up edible plants from a lake bottom.

A **moose** can keep his head **underwater** for a whole minute before coming up for air! **Moose** have long legs. Their front legs are longer than their back legs. Long front legs help **moose** jump over logs in the forest.

   The black bear prefers to live in the heavily forested parts of North America. It can be found as far south as Mexico and Florida and as far north as Alaska and Canada. In the United States, black bears live in forty-one out of fifty states. Due to their disappearing habitat, sometimes black bears will wander into people's backyards and even use their swimming pools!

A baby bear is called a cub. When a baby bear is born, it is only as big as a stick of butter. Bear cubs love to play, but they never play far from their mother.

The **grizzly** bear lives in the northwestern portion of the United States and Alaska. If you visit Yellowstone National Park or Grand Teton National Park, you may be able to spot one of these creatures. As awesome as they are, they can be very dangerous, making it extremely important to keep all food in a bear proof can. These special cans will prevent bears from searching for food in your campground.

 **Grizzly** bears like to eat fish, but they also eat other animals including moose, sheep and deer. Bears also eat grass, roots and berries.

James Hautman ©

Bighorn sheep live in mountainous regions such as Alaska, Idaho, California and throughout the Rocky Mountains. These animals are so nimble they can walk along a steep mountain ledge not much wider than a circus tightrope!

Bighorn sheep have horns, not antlers. Deer and moose have antlers. Horns are never shed, while antlers are shed every year.

The words sheep, moose and deer have something in common. Each of these words can mean one animal or a whole herd of them!

The grey wolf used to live throughout most of North America. Now, because of human hunters and the loss of their natural habitat, the grey wolf only populates some northern areas of the United States and parts of Canada. **Wolves** live in a family unit called a wolf pack. Before they set off to hunt, wolf packs sometimes howl together.

Wolves hunt in a pack. These animals work as a team to catch their meal. They catch deer, sheep, and other large animals.

Despite looking big and fierce, the **mountain lion** is a shy creature that usually tries to stay far away from humans. These graceful big cats live in a variety of habitats, including our deserts, forests and mountains. Did you know that the **mountain lion** has other names as well? They are also called cougar, puma, and panther.

A **mountain lion** does not live in a herd and it does not hunt in a pack. It lives and hunts alone. The **mountain lion** may travel up to twenty-five miles in one night in search of prey.

Twice as big as the common housecat, the **bobcat** is a **fierce** predator that is often hunted for its beautiful lush fur. Except for our cities, **bobcats** can be found almost anywhere. They live in all four deserts of the American Southwest but also roam the mountains where water is abundant.

The **bobcat** likes to live alone, just like the mountain lion. It has a short tail, long legs and very big paws. The **bobcat** looks like a sweet kitty, but it is really very **fierce**.

The Red Fox is another animal that hunts alone. Thanks to keen ears, a red fox can actually hear mice as they creep up from their underground burrows. The red fox waits until the mouse appears and then jumps high into the air to pounce on it—just like a cat!

 The red fox can live in both hot and cold climates. Sometimes a red fox will not eat all of its food. It will bury the food. Later, the red fox can dig it up and eat it.

Mallards are wild ducks that prefer to live near shallow water. They are often found living around lakes or ponds in parks. **Mallards** are very social birds and live together in groups called flocks. Male **mallards** can be recognized by their green heads while female **mallards** are a spotted brown.

Most **mallards** fly south for the winter. In the spring, they fly north and build nests near water. The female lays eggs. The eggs hatch in about four weeks.

   Raccoons are wily creatures that live in forested areas, but are very adaptable to living just about anywhere! When human development takes away their natural habitats, raccoons will use abandoned buildings and even abandoned cars to make their homes. In their natural habitat, raccoons live in burrows or dens. Another animal that lives in a den is called a **chipmunk**.

James Hautman

Chipmunks live in the woods and can be seen in many of our parks. **Chipmunks** can carry lots of food in their cheeks. They may store the food in a tree to eat later.

Bald eagles make their home in tall trees near large bodies of water, where there are plenty of fish to eat. Not so long ago, **bald eagles** were on their way to extinction due to habitat loss, hunting and poisons like DDT. Thanks to conservation efforts, their numbers have increased significantly and they now live in almost every state. However, we still need to protect them or they may become endangered again.

   The **bald eagle** is the national bird of the United States. You can find a picture of the bald eagle on the back of many coins. Look on the back of a quarter and see if there is an **eagle**!

Wild **turkeys** can fly, but only very low to the ground, which may be the reason they do not migrate during the winter. Instead, they live year round in forests. Sometimes they can be seen in parks, including parks in **New York City**! When the United States was a very young country, Benjamin Franklin wanted to make the wild **turkey** the national bird instead of the eagle.

Some people in **New York** have seen wild **turkeys** walk across the street. Other people say they have even seen them go into buildings! **Turkeys** going for a walk in **New York City** is pretty wild!

So many different kinds of wildlife live across the vast, **wonderful** land of North America. When we respect and take care of the environment, we are also taking care of the habitats of the amazing animals that live on this land with us.

　Taking care of our water, land, and air is a **wonderful** way to take care of our wild animals too.

If you liked **Wild Animals of the United States**, here is another We Both Read® Book you are sure to enjoy!

Endangered Animals

This book takes a close look at various animals from around the world that are in danger of becoming extinct. It discusses how the animals have become endangered due to worldwide threats including pollution, deforestation and global warming. Featuring stunning photographs of many endangered animals in their natural habitats, the book also relates some of the positive steps being taken to protect the animals and explains how we can all take part in saving them.